100 YEARS OF GOLF

100 YEARS OF GOLF

PA Photos

AMMONITE
PRESS

First published 2008 by

AMMONITE PRESS

an imprint of AE Publications Ltd,
166 High Street, Lewes, East Sussex BN7 1XU

ISBN 978-1-906672-04-1

British Cataloguing in Publication Data. A catalogue record of this book is available from the British Library.

Editor **NEIL DUNNICLIFFE**
Designer **JO PATTERSON**

Colour origination by GMC Reprographics
Printed and bound by Colorprint Offset in China

Contents

Chapter One
PEOPLE

GOLFING HEROES

As the 20th century dawned on the fairways and greens of the British Isles, three players dominated the world of golf

John Henry (J.H.) Taylor, Harry Vardon and James Braid were called the 'Great Triumvirate'.

While on an exhibition tour in 1900 Vardon landed the US Open using the 'Vardon Flyer' golf ball. He was considered a great ambassador for the game and it was that tour which is said to have spurred interest in golf in America. He was the first player to win both Opens.

Taylor, meanwhile, played until well into his fifties and became one of the driving forces behind the formation of the Professional Golfers Association (PGA) in Britain. After he retired, course design became the great passion for Braid and it is estimated that he was involved in the building, or redesign, of over 200 of them.

Certainly worthy of ranking alongside them are John Ball Junior, Abe Mitchell and Edward 'Ted' Ray whose achieve-

ments seemed sometimes to be overshadowed by the great threesome.

Ball won the Amateur title, which was considered one of the top tournaments, eight times and also captured the British Open, the first amateur to do so, in 1890. He continued to play competitive golf until he retired after taking part in the 1921 Amateur Open. Mitchell was acknowledged as the greatest striker of a ball in his era. Ray was captain of the Great Britain & Ireland team that played against the United States in 1926, spawning the Ryder Cup.

The sport was beginning to grab the interest also of the big manufacturing companies and it was at the start of the century that Goodrich Rubber patented a machine for winding the rubber threads around the core of a Haskell ball. Mass production soon followed.

A couple of years later Scottish golfer Sandy Herd was the first player to use the Haskell to win both the Hoylake (England) Open and the British Open. His appearances in the latter tournament spanned 50 years with his last being at the venerable age of 71 in 1939.

It was in the first decade of the new century that women's golf began to take off and in 1908 Mrs Gordon Robertson became the first female professional.

As the First World War loomed Harry Vardon won his sixth Open, while Walter Hagen was the new rising star from across the Atlantic and he marked the beginning of the professional golfer.

THE 1920s

With the arrival of the 1920s, Jock Hutchison, born in Scotland, became the first US-based golfer to land Britain's major title. To achieve the feat he used deep-grooved irons, which were to be banned four years later.

The 1920s also saw the birth of the Walker Cup, for amateurs, and the Ryder Cup, for the pros, as biennial team competitions between Great Britain & Ireland and America. The names that reverberated around the amateur ranks during the 1920s were those of Joyce and Roger Wethered, with the former being widely regarded as the greatest British woman player of her time.

THE 1930s AND 1940s

It took until the late 1930s before the amateurs could defeat the Americans in the Walker Cup but their professional counterparts achieved victory in the second event in 1929 at a cold and snowy Moortown Golf Club in Leeds when captain George Duncan, who had won the first post-war Open in 1920, lifted the Ryder Cup. One of Duncan's teammates that year was a young Henry Cotton who went on to

OPPOSITE

HARRY VARDON. 1920

BELOW

SAM SNEAD. 30/09/1953

dominate British golf during the 1930s and 1940s. He won his first contest at the age of 16 in 1923 and promptly turned professional a year later along with his brother Leslie.

The last pre-war Open was held at St Andrews and victory went to Richard 'Dick' Burton. He is best remembered for holding the Open title for the longest time because of the intervening war years.

AFTER THE WAR

As the world tried to return to normal Cotton won the last of his three Open titles in 1948. He served as captain in the Ryder Cup the year before and would do so again six years later.

During this period the US had its own great triumvirate in Ben Hogan, Byron Nelson and Sam Snead – and it was in the States that golf was televised for the first time, when the 1947 US Open was broadcast.

When the Second World War ended, Max Faulkner's career started and he was one of the game's most flamboyant characters, regularly attired in colourful clothes, such as salmon pink plus fours.

THE 1950s AND 1960s

It was during this era that the career of Neil Coles began. Coles is the only man to win a professional golf tournament in six different decades. His first victory came in 1956 and his last in 2002 when he won the Lawrence Batley Seniors tournament at the age of 67.

In the 1960s, improvements in trans-Atlantic travel saw more American golfers crossing the ocean. The decade also saw the emergence of Scunthorpe-born Tony Jacklin as a major force in golf, as he would continue to be well into the 1970s.

THE 1970s

In 1970 Peter Oosterhuis looked to be the next brightest star on the horizon, following a distinguished amateur career representing Britain in the Walker Cup and Eisenhower Trophy.

The Londoner went on to finish runner-up in the Open on two occasions and won the European Order of Merit title four years in a row (1971 to 1974 inclusive). He played in the Ryder Cup six times from 1971 to 1981 and among the famous scalps he took were those of Arnold Palmer and Johnny Miller.

Like Oosterhuis, Essex-born Michael Bonallack had a brilliant career in the unpaid ranks, winning the Amateur Championship five times. When he finally put his clubs down from competitive playing he became one of the sport's leading administrators and was knighted in 1998.

England's Trevor Homer and Peter McEvoy each won the Amateur title

twice in the 1970s. The decade also saw the first metal woods.

THE 1980s ONWARDS

In the 1980s there was another major resurgence for British golf through the exploits of Nick Faldo, Sandy Lyle and Ian Woosnam. Hertfordshire-born Faldo first took up the game when he borrowed some clubs from a neighbour after watching American Jack Nicklaus play the 1971 US Masters on TV. He won the English Amateur title while working as a carpet fitter. After turning pro he became, at the time, the youngest golfer to play in the Ryder Cup and was considered the best golfer in the world.

Although born in Shrewsbury, Lyle went to live in Scotland when his father became resident professional at the Hawkstone Park golf club. He topped the Merit table three times, including twice in the 1980s.

OPPOSITE
TONY JACKLIN IN ACTION. 12/07/1969

ABOVE
NICK FALDO. 25/06/1977

Woosnam's career took off in 1982 after he won the Swiss Open and he reached the top of the tree in 1991 when he was officially ranked No.1 in the world.

One of the first British golfers to go to a US college was Colin Montgomerie who burst upon the scene when he was named the European Tour's Rookie of the Year in 1988. A year later he won his first title by eight shots and made his Ryder Cup debut in 1991. Between 1993 and 1999 he set the record for the most Order of Merit titles won and at the height of his powers he reached second in the world rankings.

The 1990s also witnessed the arrival of Darren Clarke and Lee Westwood who would go on to be the mainstays in the Ryder Cup throughout the decade and into the 21st century. Justin Rose burst to prominence in the 1998 Open when finishing fourth as a 17 year old amateur. Four years later he won his first professional tournament.

Just as the century had started with a British victory in the Open, so it closed the same way with Scotsman Paul Lawrie winning the 1999 Open at Carnoustie in Angus, Ayrshire. Another Scottish course, Nairn on the shores of the Moray Firth, was host to a British victory with Peter McEvoy leading the amateurs to victory in the Walker Cup.

Golf is an international sport, and many of the great moments in British golf have come from players from around the world. This book also features many of the key international characters who have contributed to the game in Britain, including Walter Hagen, Ben Hogan, Arnold Palmer, Jack Nicklaus, Gary Player, Seve Ballesteros, Greg Norman and Tiger Woods.

HAROLD HILTON. 1895

JOHNNY LAIDLAY. 1895

(L-R) MRS KENNIN, MISS CAMPBELL, MRS SIMSTER AND MISS THOMPSON. 1906

JAMES BRAID DRIVES A GUTTIE FROM THE TEE IN A MATCH TO DETERMINE THE RELATIVE VALUES OF THE TWO TYPES OF BALL – THE GUTTIES AND THE RUBBER CORES. J.H. TAYLOR (L) LOOKS ON. 1909

TOM VARDON WITH HIS CADDY RAY DURING THE OPEN CHAMPIONSHIP HELD AT THE ROYAL CINQUE PORTS GOLF CLUB IN DEAL, KENT. 23/07/1909

MRS WILCOCK. 1912

HAROLD HILTON (R) DRIVES, WATCHED BY HIS OPPONENT FRANCIS OUIMET (SIXTH L). 10/10/1913

JOYCE WETHERED. 1920

HARRY VARDON IN ACTION. 17/10/1921

JIM BARNES (L) AND WALTER HAGEN (R). 01/06/1923

WALTER HAGEN PLAYS TO THE 10TH GREEN. 12/07/1924

ARTHUR HAVERS (SECOND R). 01/06/1928

GEORGE DUNCAN PLAYS FROM AN AWKWARD LIE AT THE SIXTH. THE ONLY SPECTATOR WITH HIS EYES ON DUNCAN AND NOT THE BALL IS FORMER BRITISH HEAVYWEIGHT BOXING CHAMPION, BOMBARDIER BILLY WELLS. 10/04/1929

SAMUEL RYDER, DONOR OF THE
RYDER CUP. 01/03/1930

ENGLAND'S ABE MITCHELL (L) AND GEORGE DUNCAN (R) LINE UP ALONGSIDE THEIR OPPONENTS, USA'S WALTER HAGEN (SECOND L) AND JIM BARNES (SECOND R), BEFORE THE START OF THE MATCH. 12/06/1930

BOBBY JONES IN ACTION. 20/06/1930

CECIL LEITCH (R) IN PLAY. 07/04/1933

MEMBERS OF THE GREAT BRITAIN RYDER CUP TEAM, WHO PLAYED A COMPETITION TO COMMEMORATE THE 10TH ANNIVERSARY OF THE OPENING OF RICHMOND PUBLIC COURSE: (BACK ROW, L-R) ARTHUR HAVERS, SYD EASTERBROOK, ALLAN DAILEY, ALF PADGHAM; (FRONT ROW, L-R) ALF PERRY, ARTHUR LACEY, PERCY ALLISS, NON-PLAYING CAPTAIN JH TAYLOR, ABE MITCHELL, CHARLES WHITCOMBE. 10/06/1933

(L-R) TED RAY, C.K. COTTON, M.C. PARK, S.S. FIELD. 18/03/1935

OPPOSITE

HAROLD HILTON. 25/10/1933

DICK BURTON. 13/04/1948

SAM KING DRIVES FROM THE FIRST TEE. 21/04/1949

HENRY COTTON TEES OFF, WATCHED BY A LARGE GALLERY. 23/07/1949

MILDRED 'BABE' ZAHARIAS (L) STROLLS DOWN THE FAIRWAY WITH HER PLAYING PARTNER. 12/06/1951

HARRY BRADSHAW. 17/04/1952

PETER ALLISS. 18/04/1952

HARRY WEETMAN (R). 25/06/1952

REGULAR VISITOR TO BRITAIN, BOB HOPE TRIES PLAYING A SHOT IN ALTERNATIVE HEADGEAR. 24/09/1953

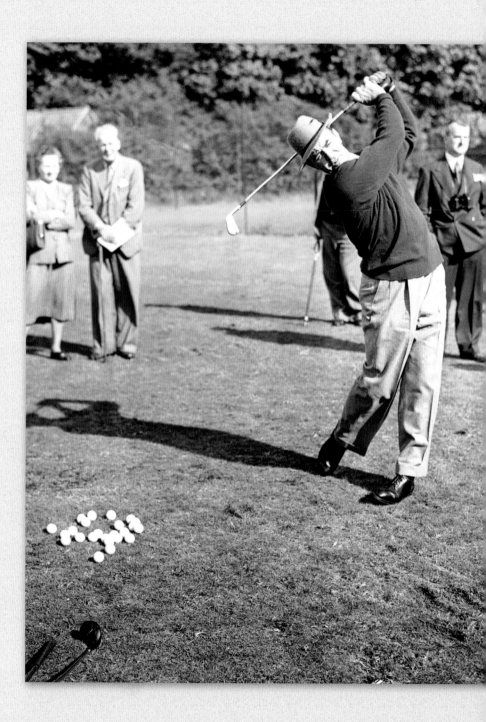

SAM SNEAD PRACTISES. 28/09/1953

GREAT BRITAIN'S FRED DALY LOFTS THE BALL ONTO THE GREEN. 03/10/1953

HUGH BOYLE PLAYS OFF WATCHED BY (L-R) J.H. ELLIS, F. GOULD AND P.D. HEDGES. 10/05/1954

THE USA TEAM: (L-R) JOE PATTON, JOE CONRAD, DON CHERRY, RICHARD YOST, W. CAMPBELL, E. HARVIE WARD, JAMES JACKSON, DALE MOREY, BRUCE CUDD. 13/05/1955

HENRY COTTON DURING THE SECOND DAY OF THE DUNLOP MASTERS TOURNAMENT AT LITTLE ASTON. 22/09/1955

THE USA'S BEN HOGAN IN ACTION. 21/06/1956

BRUCE CRAMPTON (L) IN
CONVERSATION WITH RICHARD
BURTON (R). 24/04/1957

CHRISTY O'CONNOR SENIOR (R) DRIVES FROM THE FIRST TEE, WATCHED BY PETER ALLISS (L). 26/04/1957

GREAT BRITAIN'S KEN BOUSFIELD SHOWERS SAND AS HE PLAYS OUT OF A BUNKER AT THE FIFTH IN ONE OF THE OPENING MATCHES OF THE RYDER CUP TOURNAMENT AT LINDRICK, SHEFFIELD. 05/10/1957

OPPOSITE

MAX FAULKNER PLAYS A SHOT OUT OF A BED OF DAFFODILS. 23/04/1958

BOBBY LOCKE TEES OFF. 06/05/1958

PETER THOMSON. 09/09/1958

NORMAN DREW (R) PLAYS A SHOT WATCHED BY KEITH MACDONALD (L). 24/08/1960

ARNOLD PALMER AT ROYAL BIRKDALE PREPARING FOR THE OPEN. 10/07/1961

AMERICA'S JACK NICKLAUS IN ACTION. 01/01/1962

HENRY COTTON WITH HIS CLUBS. 01/06/1962

PETER ALLISS TEES OFF. 15/06/1963

OPPOSITE

BOBBY LOCKE TEES OFF. 07/06/1962

ARNOLD PALMER. 11/07/1963

OPPOSITE

PATTY BERG IN ACTION. 28/08/1963

PATTY BERG SHOWS OFF HER WILSON
BALLS. 28/08/1963

ARNOLD PALMER PUTTING ON THE 16TH GREEN. 10/10/1964

USA'S SAM SNEAD PLAYS OUT OF THE ROUGH. 05/07/1965

TONY LEMA PLAYS OUT OF A BUNKER. 15/10/1965

SAM SNEAD PUTTING. 01/07/1966

JACK NICKLAUS PUTTING ON THE FIFTH GREEN AT THE OPEN CHAMPIONSHIP AT MUIRFIELD. 08/07/1966

JACK NICKLAUS PLAYS A SHOT FROM
THE BUNKER. 07/10/1966

AMERICAN DOUG SANDERS SHOWS
HIS RELIEF AS HIS PUTT GOES IN ON
THE 17TH GREEN. 05/10/1967

GARY PLAYER. 12/10/1967

ARNOLD PALMER IN ACTION. 12/10/1967

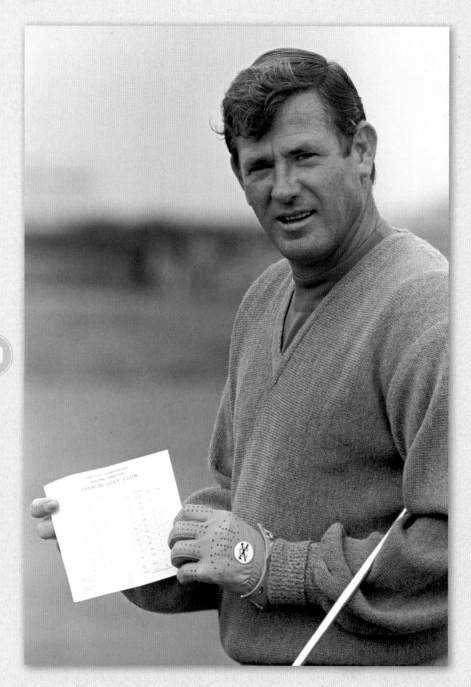

DOUG SANDERS. 10/07/1968

LEE TREVINO (L) AND TONY JACKLIN (R) WALK TO THE NEXT HOLE TOGETHER. 11/10/1968

CATHERINE LACOSTE. 20/03/1969

EDDIE POLLAND EYES UP A PUTT. 30/05/1969

GARY PLAYER DRIVING. 01/07/1969

TONY JACKLIN PLAYING OUT OF THE ROUGH ON THE FOURTH GREEN, DURING THE OPEN CHAMPIONSHIP AT ROYAL LYTHAM & ST ANNES. 11/07/1969

ENGLAND'S TONY JACKLIN IN ACTION. 11/07/1969

OPPOSITE

GARY PLAYER. 12/07/1969

JACK NICKLAUS. 09/10/1970

LEE TREVINO PLAYS OUT OF A BUNKER. 08/07/1971

LIANG HUAN LU LOOKS PLEASED WITH HIS SECOND ROUND 70. 08/07/1971

TONY JACKLIN PLAYS OUT OF A BUNKER. 05/09/1971

ARNOLD PALMER PLAYS OUT OF A BUNKER. 07/10/1971

OPPOSITE

GARY PLAYER PLAYS OUT OF A BUNKER. 07/10/1971

AMERICAN VETERAN GENE SARAZEN ADMIRES THE BALL WITH WHICH HE HOLED OUT IN ONE AT THE 126-YARD EIGHTH IN THE OPEN CHAMPIONSHIP AT TROON. A FORMER TITLE HOLDER, HE WAS THEN 71 AND THE OLDEST PLAYER IN THE COMPETITION. 11/07/1973

SANDY LYLE, 16, THE YOUNGEST
COMPETITOR IN THE OPEN
CHAMPIONSHIP HELD AT ROYAL
LYTHAM & ST ANNES. 09/07/1974

AMERICAN TOM WATSON AT THE OPEN CHAMPIONSHIP AT CARNOUSTIE. 01/07/1975

JACK NICKLAUS IN ACTION. 01/03/1976

GARY PLAYER TEEING OFF. 31/05/1976

ARNOLD PALMER LINES UP A PUTT. 07/07/1976

ARNOLD PALMER PLAYS A SHOT OUT
OF THE ROUGH. 07/07/1976

JOHNNY MILLER RELAXES. 10/07/1976

SEVE BALLESTEROS IN ACTION DURING THE LAST ROUND OF THE OPEN CHAMPIONSHIP, AT ROYAL BIRKDALE. 10/07/1976

JACK NICKLAUS ON THE FAIRWAY.

01/08/1976

GARY PLAYER IN ACTION. 07/07/1977

ARNOLD PALMER DRIVING. 07/07/1977

JACK NICKLAUS LINING UP A PUTT. 07/07/1977

JACK NICKLAUS IN ACTION. 10/07/1977

DEBBIE AUSTIN AND HER CADDY TAKE
A BREAK. 04/08/1977

(L-R) GREAT BRITAIN AND IRELAND'S BRIAN BARNES AND BERNARD GALLACHER CAN'T BEAR TO LOOK AS THE USA TEAM
WIN ANOTHER POINT. 17/09/1977

ENGLAND'S TONY JACKLIN, WATCHED BY USA'S JACK NICKLAUS, PLACES HIS BALL TO PUTT. 09/10/1977

JACK NICKLAUS IN ACTION. 10/10/1977

TOM WATSON LOOKS HAPPY WITH HIS FIRST ROUND SCORE OF 68 (3 UNDER). 17/07/1980

OPPOSITE

NANCY LOPEZ HOLDS HER GLOVE IN HER MOUTH AS SHE WAITS TO CATCH A
GOLF BALL. 04/08/1979

TOM WATSON IN ACTION. 20/07/1980

GARY PLAYER IN ACTION
AT ROYAL ST GEORGE'S. 07/07/1981

ARNOLD PALMER IN ACTION AT ROYAL ST GEORGE'S. 07/07/1981

GREG NORMAN (L) AND SEVE BALLESTEROS (R) WATCH NORMAN'S DRIVE FROM THE FOURTH TEE. 18/07/1981

JACK NICKLAUS (L) TALKS TO GARY PLAYER (R). 18/07/1981

LEE TREVINO. 18/07/1981

GREG NORMAN, AUSTRALIA.
26/09/1981

ARNOLD PALMER. 1982

TONY JACKLIN (L) AND JACK NICKLAUS (R). 1982

OPPOSITE

BERNARD GALLACHER LINES UP A
PUTT. 06/07/1982

HUBERT GREEN LINES UP A PUTT.

17/07/1982

GRAHAM MARSH. 27/07/1982

TONY JACKLIN CHIPS OUT OF A BUNKER. 23/09/1982

NICK FALDO LINES UP A PUTT.

14/10/1982

GREG NORMAN. 22/07/1984

IAN WOOSNAM CELEBRATES. 12/07/1985

EUROPE'S PAUL WAY PRACTISES HIS
BUNKER SHOTS. 12/09/1985

EUROPE'S SANDY LYLE (TOP) AND
KEN BROWN LINE UP A PUTT ON THE
FIFTH GREEN. 13/09/1985

TOM WATSON. 14/07/1987

OPPOSITE

NICK FALDO RESTS HIS LEGS AFTER
SCORING A THREE UNDER PAR 68 IN
THE FIRST ROUND OF THE OPEN
CHAMPIONSHIP. 16/07/1987

IAN WOOSNAM (R) AND HIS CADDY PHIL MORBEY (L) SURVEY THE FAIRWAY. 19/10/1987

SANDY LYLE (L) AND NICK FALDO (R)
TRY SKIMMING GOLF BALLS IN ONE
OF THE MANY PUDDLES AT
WENTWORTH, WHERE PLAY WAS
POSTPONED DUE TO TORRENTIAL
RAIN. 09/10/1988

SEVE BALLESTEROS (L) AND JOSE MARIA OLAZABAL (R). 1990

PAUL AZINGER, USA, CELEBRATES A
SUCCESSFUL PUTT. 11/06/1990

SANDY LYLE. 16/10/1992

NICK FALDO DURING HIS PRACTICE ROUND AT THE OPEN TOURNAMENT AT ROYAL ST GEORGE'S. 13/07/1993

BERNHARD LANGER AND IAN
WOOSNAM CONTEMPLATE THE NEXT
SHOT. 23/09/1993

SEVE BALLESTEROS PLAYS A BUNKER SHOT. 23/09/1993

EUROPE'S PETER BAKER (L) AND BARRY LANE (R). 25/09/1993

RONAN RAFFERTY, NORTHERN IRELAND. 29/05/1995

TOM WATSON. 20/07/1995

BERNHARD LANGER CELEBRATES.

22/09/1995

JESPER PARNEVIK, SWEDEN. 19/07/1996

GREG NORMAN, AUSTRALIA. 18/07/1997

BRIAN WATTS PLAYS OUT OF A
BUNKER AT THE 18TH, WATCHED BY A
CAMERAMAN. 19/07/1998

JUSTIN ROSE WATCHES HIS TEE SHOT
FROM THE SECOND. 19/07/1998

JEAN VAN DE VELDE HITS OUT OF A
BUNKER ON THE SECOND GREEN.
18/07/1999

JEAN VAN DE VELDE STANDING IN THE BROOK AFTER PUTTING HIS BALL INTO THE WATER ON THE 18TH. 18/07/1999

JUSTIN LEONARD CELEBRATES WINNING THE RYDER CUP FOR AMERICA. 26/09/1999

TIGER WOODS TEES OFF. 19/07/2000

IAN POULTER SHOWS OFF HIS EYE-CATCHING HAIRCUT DURING A PRACTICE ROUND. 22/07/2003

OPPOSITE

PAUL MCGINLEY CELEBRATES WINNING THE RYDER CUP. 29/09/2002

JOHN DALY WATCHES A DRIVE. 12/07/2005

TIGER WOODS. 17/07/2005

USA'S MICHELLE WIE. 28/07/2005

ENGLAND'S LAURA DAVIES. 30/07/2005

SCOTLAND'S COLIN MONTGOMERIE DURING THE FINAL ROUND OF THE DUNHILL LINKS CHAMPIONSHIPS AT ST ANDREWS. 2/10/2005

OPPOSITE

JULI INKSTER LINES UP A PUTT WITH HER CADDY DURING THE FIRST ROUND OF THE WEETABIX WOMEN'S OPEN AT ROYAL LYTHAM & ST ANNES. 03/08/2006

ENGLAND'S PAUL CASEY CHIPS OUT OF A BUNKER DURING THE HSBC WORLD MATCH PLAY CHAMPIONSHIP AT WENTWORTH. 15/09/2006

USA RYDER CUP PLAYERS, JIM FURYK (L) AND TIGER WOODS, ON THE PRACTICE GREEN, PRIOR TO THEIR FINAL PRACTICE ROUND AT THE K CLUB, CO KILDARE, IRELAND, AHEAD OF THE RYDER CUP WHICH OFFICIALLY STARTED WITH THE OPENING CEREMONY LATER THAT DAY. 21/09/2006

MARK CALCAVECCHIA IN ACTION DURING A PRACTICE DAY AHEAD OF THE OPEN CHAMPIONSHIP AT CARNOUSTIE.
18/07/2007

OPPOSITE

PAUL MCGINLEY TREATS HIMSELF TO AN ICE CREAM DURING A PRACTICE DAY
AHEAD OF THE OPEN CHAMPIONSHIP AT CARNOUSTIE. 17/07/2007

Chapter Two
PLACES

A GOOD WALK...

American writer Mark Twain once remarked that golf was a good walk spoiled. He may have changed his mind if he could have seen some of the spectacular settings and scenery, along with the history, that make up the courses where the game is played in the British Isles

Scotland has always been synonymous with the sport, with Bruntsfield Links near Edinburgh staking claim to being the oldest course in the world dating back to the mid-15th century.

But it's St Andrews on the Fife coast that is considered the home of golf and it is from there that the Royal and Ancient Club set the rules worldwide (except in America and Mexico). It's the most used course for the Open Championship, considered the major tournament in the golfing world.

All the venues for the event are links courses set along the coasts of Britain, although Muirfield in East Lothian is slightly different in that it is upon elevated ancient land claimed from the sea. It has a sandy base and small sea shells are found in the bunkers around the course. It is home to the world's oldest golf club, the 'Honourable Company of Edinburgh Golfers', which was formed in 1744.

One of the most spectacular courses in Scotland is Turnberry, which is set on the Atlantic coast in South Ayrshire right next to the Irish Sea. It has superb views across to the Isles of Mull and Arran and is unusual for a links course because there are no dunes protecting the holes that run close to the sea. It was founded in 1902 but came close to extinction twice as it was requisitioned during both World Wars and used as an airbase. During the Second World War runways were built on some of the holes and it wasn't until 1951 that the course was able to re-open following two years of extensive renovation.

Just along the coast from Turnberry is Royal Troon where the longest and shortest holes in Open Championship golf can be found. The par three eighth hole, known as the 'Postage Stamp', is just 123yds long and is regarded as one of the top holes in the world, while the par five sixth ('Turnberry') is just over 600yds. One of the toughest courses in the world is Carnoustie in Angus.

Probably one of the remotest courses in the British Isles is Royal Dornoch, which is located 50 miles north of Inverness. During summer it stays so light there that play has been known to go on until midnight.

NORTH WEST ENGLAND

Moving back over the border, the second oldest seaside links course in England is Royal Liverpool at Hoylake, which was founded in 1869. It was originally built on the site of a racecourse and is unusually flat with three sides of the course being bordered by houses, while the Dee Estuary lies on the western side.

Staying in the north west, situated on the Southport sands is Royal Birkdale. It has hosted the Open eight times but as yet no player from the United Kingdom has won the tournament there.

ROYAL LYTHAM & ST ANNES

Just 10 miles down the road is the most northerly of the English championship courses, Royal Lytham & St Annes. It is about a mile inland, but Blackpool Tower is clearly visible in the distance. Like Hoylake it is surrounded by houses but has the railway line on its western side. It is unique amongst championship courses in that the first hole is a par three.

KENT COURSES

Heading south and into Kent there are three courses that had an influence on British golf. Royal St George's in Sandwich is where the first Open championship outside Scotland was played in 1894. Royal St George's has hosted the Open 13 times in total, more than any other English course. It is home to the deepest bunker in golf, the 'Himalayas'.

On the same stretch of coastline is the Prince's Golf Club, which along with Royal Portrush in Northern Ireland, is one of only two clubs to have hosted the Open just once. The

During the War he had to make an emergency landing by the fourth tee after his Spitfire limped home after being crippled over northern France.

Running along the coast of Sandwich Bay is the Royal Cinque Ports Club near to the town of Deal. It was host to two Opens in 1909 and 1920.

COURSES IN WALES

In Wales are two of the more interesting courses, in the county of Powys. Glynneath Golf Club is one, while former Ryder Cup captain and US Masters winner Ian Woosnam learnt the game at Llanymynech, near Oswestry. This has the distinction of being the only course in the world with holes in two countries. Fifteen are in Wales and three over the border in Shropshire, England.

Royal Porthcawl in Glamorgan may not be a place that Tiger Woods will want to remember in a hurry. As an amateur he represented the US there in the Walker Cup match of 1995 against Great Britain but was beaten at the last hole by Gary Wolstenholme.

original layout was completed in 1906 and a year later former Prime Minster A. J. Balfour drove the first ball in the Founder's Vase.

One of the most famous sons of Prince's is Second World War ace Percy Belgrave 'Laddie' Lucas, who was actually born in the clubhouse.

The latter went on to win the Lagonda Trophy played at one of the oldest courses in East Anglia, the wonderfully named Gog Magog Golf Club in Cambridgeshire.

SURREY

Down in Surrey, the West Course at Wentworth is probably the most televised in Britain as it hosts three professional tournaments every year: the World Match Play; PGA Championship; and the Seniors Masters. It also hosted the fiercely contested 1953 Ryder Cup battle between teams from Great Britain and the United States, which the latter won by a single point.

As the Second World War began the Army requisitioned the clubhouse and numerous underground bunkers were built. The fairways were also allowed to grow wild as the authorities feared that enemy aircraft might land on them.

Another Surrey course to host the Ryder Cup is Walton Heath, which staged the 1981 renewal when the US

squad beat the European side. The course was opened in 1904 when its resident professional was James Braid of the 'Great Triumvirate'. He held that post until 1950.

SUNNINGDALE

Just across the border in Berkshire is Sunningdale, which has the unusual attraction of a halfway hut, which apparently serves a very fine sausage sandwich. Another place where players can get decent refreshments is at the clubhouse at Royal North Devon, the oldest course in England still playing along its original fairways and also the first links track to be laid outside Scotland.

Vying with Sunningdale for the title of best inland course in the British Isles is Woodhall Spa in Lincolnshire. It was originally laid out by Harry Vardon, opened for play in 1905 and is now the home of the English Golf Union.

OPPOSITE
PAUL WAY PLAYS A SHOT FROM THE 15TH FAIRWAY AT ROYAL ST GEORGE'S. 13/07/1993

LEFT
ERNIE ELS AT WENTWORTH. 13/10/2007

THE FINAL PUTT FROM BOBBY JONES (L) IN FRONT OF THE CLUBHOUSE TO WIN THE OPEN CHAMPIONSHIP AT ROYAL
LYTHAM & ST ANNES. 26/06/1926

DOUGLAS FAIRBANKS WAS DEFEATED BY ONE HOLE BY J.R. ABERCROMBIE IN THE FIRST ROUND OF THE BRITISH AMATEUR CHAMPIONSHIP. A LARGE GALLERY, INCLUDING MANY GIRLS, FOLLOWED HIM AROUND THE COURSE. PICTURE SHOWS DOUGLAS FAIRBANKS WALKING OVER THE BRIDGE TO THE 18TH GREEN. 19/05/1931

MRS A.C. JOHNSTON (L) AND MISS H. JOANNIDES (R) WALK OVER THE BRIDGE DURING THEIR ROUND IN THE LADIES' GOLF UNION INTERNATIONAL GOLD CUP AT RANELAGH CLUB, BARNES. 19/04/1932

MISS GWEN CRADOCK-HARTOPP PLAYS A STROKE TO A GALLERY OF GEESE AT RANELAGH CLUB, BARNES. 10/04/1935

TWO SPECTATORS WATCH FROM THE BANK AS FRANCIS RICARDO PLAYS OUT OF A BUNKER BY THE SIXTH GREEN AT ROYAL ST GEORGE'S. 26/05/1937

A LARGE GALLERY WATCHES SAM SNEAD PRACTISE HIS PUTTING AT WENTWORTH. 30/09/1953

GARY PLAYER TEES OFF AT THE FOURTH AT SUNNINGDALE. 04/05/1956

THE USA'S BEN HOGAN IN ACTION AT WENTWORTH. 21/06/1956

LEFT-HANDER LAVINIA MARTIN, OF THE PYECOMBE GOLF CLUB, SUSSEX, SHOWS FELLOW MEMBER HENRY LONGHURST A SET OF GOLF CLUBS SENT TO HER FROM AMERICA. 09/08/1958

AMERICAN ARNOLD PALMER LOOKS ON AS HIS CADDIE FISHES FOR HIS BALL IN ONE OF THE LARGE POOLS OF WATER LEFT BY OVERNIGHT RAINSTORMS ON THE SIXTH FAIRWAY OF THE ROYAL BIRKDALE GOLF COURSE, LANCASHIRE. 13/07/1961

OPEN CHAMPION BOB CHARLES MAKES A SPEECH AFTER BEING PRESENTED WITH THE CLARET JUG AT ROYAL LYTHAM & ST ANNES. 13/07/1963

AMERICAN TONY LEMA WATCHES HIS PUTT LIP THE HOLE FOR A 68, ON THE SECOND DAY OF THE OPEN AT ST ANDREWS.

09/07/1964

NEIL COLES PUTTING ON THE THIRD GREEN AT WENTWORTH. 09/10/1964

OPPOSITE
ARNOLD PALMER (L) LOOKS ON AS GARY PLAYER (R) PUTTS ON THE 16TH GREEN
AT WENTWORTH. 10/10/1964

JACK NICKLAUS CHIPS OUT OF THE ROUGH AT WENTWORTH. 08/10/1966

TONY JACKLIN PLAYS A SHOT FROM UNDERNEATH THE STAND DURING THE OPEN AT ROYAL LYTHAM & ST ANNES.

12/07/1969

TONY JACKLIN ACKNOWLEDGES THE CHEERS OF THE CROWD AS HE WALKS OFF THE LAST GREEN THE OPEN CHAMPION AT ROYAL LYTHAM & ST ANNES. 12/07/1969

TONY JACKLIN, FIRST BRITISH WINNER OF THE US OPEN CHAMPIONSHIP FOR 50 YEARS, RIDES IN A VINTAGE WHITE CADILLAC AT THE HEAD OF A MOTORCADE THROUGH HIS HOME TOWN OF SCUNTHORPE, LINCOLNSHIRE. 24/06/1970

TOM WEISKOPF PLAYS OUT OF A
BUNKER AT WENTWORTH. 14/10/1972

OPPOSITE

THE GREAT BRITAIN AND IRELAND TEAM ABOUT TO BOARD THE PLANE WHICH WILL TAKE THEM TO ST LOUIS, USA FOR
THE RYDER CUP: (ON STEPS, TOP-BOTTOM) JOHN GARNER, CHRISTY O'CONNOR, PETER BUTLER, HARRY BANNERMAN,
TONY JACKLIN, BRIAN HUGGETT; (FRONT, L-R) CAPTAIN ERIC BROWN, MAURICE BEMBRIDGE, BERNARD GALLACHER, PETER
OOSTERHUIS, BRIAN BARNES, PETER TOWNSEND. 09/09/1971

JACK NICKLAUS MAKES A PUTT AT TURNBERRY. 07/07/1977

(L-R) TOM WATSON PLAYS FROM THE NINTH FAIRWAY AT TURNBERRY, WATCHED BY JACK NICKLAUS AND HIS CADDIE.

11/07/1977

DRIVING FROM THE ELEVATED FIFTH TEE AT COTTESMORE GOLF CLUB, PEASE POTTAGE, SUSSEX. 01/02/1980

ROYAL TROON. 1982

HUBERT GREEN LOFTS THE BALL TOWARDS THE GREEN AT ROYAL TROON. 17/07/1982

USA'S MARK O'MEARA TEES OFF FROM THE FIRST AT THE BELFRY, SUTTON COLDFIELD, AS EUROPE CAPTAIN TONY JACKLIN LOOKS ON. 14/09/1985

NICK FALDO PLAYS A SHOT AT THE OPEN CHAMPIONSHIP AT MUIRFIELD. 18/07/1987

IAN BAKER-FINCH, AUSTRALIA, IN FRONT OF THE ROYAL AND ANCIENT CLUBHOUSE. 16/10/1992

NICK FALDO TESTS THE FACILITIES DURING THE OPEN. 18/07/1993

OPPOSITE

BARRY LANE AND PETER BAKER ON
THE 10TH GREEN AT THE BELFRY.
24/09/1993

EUROPE'S COLIN MONTGOMERIE AND NICK FALDO THINK ABOUT A PUTT ON THE 10TH GREEN AT THE BELFRY. 25/09/1993

NICK FALDO TEES OFF AT THE NINTH HOLE AT TURNBERRY. 13/07/1994

GOLFERS STRIDE ALONG A FAIRWAY. 10/11/1996

GREG NORMAN PUTTS ON THE SEVENTH GREEN WITH LOCH LOMOND BEHIND. 11/07/1997

MARK O'MEARA HITS HIS SHOT TO THE 13TH GREEN AT ROYAL BIRKDALE. 16/07/1998

LEE WESTWOOD PUTTING ON THE

12TH HOLE AT SLALEY HALL. 24/06/1999

IRELAND'S PADRAIG HARRINGTON LINES UP HIS PUTT ON THE 14TH GREEN DURING THE SMURFIT EUROPEAN OPEN GOLF CHAMPIONSHIP AT THE K CLUB, CO KILDARE, IRELAND. 06/07/2001

PEOPLE WATCH FROM A WINDOW AS AMERICA'S TIGER WOODS CHIPS ONTO THE NINTH GREEN DURING THE OPEN CHAMPIONSHIP AT ROYAL LYTHAM & ST ANNES. 21/07/2001

ANDREW COLTART ON THE FAIRWAY ON THE FIRST HOLE AT WENTWORTH. 23/05/2002

TOM WATSON, USA, TEES OFF AT THE SIXTH WITH THE MOUNTAINS OF MOURNE IN THE BACKGROUND ON DAY TWO OF THE SENIOR BRITISH OPEN AT ROYAL COUNTY DOWN IN NEWCASTLE, NORTHERN IRELAND. 26/07/2002

AUSTRALIA'S KARRIE WEBB WALKS ONTO THE 18TH GREEN PAST THE SCOREBOARD DURING THE FINAL DAY OF THE WOMEN'S BRITISH OPEN AT TURNBERRY. 11/08/2002

USA'S JEFF SLUMAN (BOTTOM) PLAYS OUT OF THE BUNKER AT THE 10TH HOLE, DURING THE SECOND ROUND OF THE AMERICAN EXPRESS CHAMPIONSHIP, AT MOUNT JULIET GOLF COURSE, CO KILKENNY, REPUBLIC OF IRELAND. 20/09/2002

PREPARATIONS GET UNDER WAY FOR THE START OF THE RYDER CUP AT THE BELFRY. 23/09/2002

THE RYDER CUP TROPHY AT THE BELFRY. 25/09/2002

PAUL MCGINLEY IN THE LAKE ON THE 18TH AT THE BELFRY. 29/09/2002

CROWDS GATHER TO WATCH THE THIRD ROUND OF THE BARCLAYS SCOTTISH OPEN AT LOCH LOMOND. 12/07/2003

A GREENKEEPER PREPARES THE SIXTH HOLE FOR PRACTICE DAY, AT THE BARCLAYS SCOTTISH OPEN AT LOCH LOMOND.
07/07/2004

THE CLARET JUG AWARDED TO THE WINNER OF THE OPEN CHAMPIONSHIP RESTING ON THE BRIDGE ON THE 18TH
FAIRWAY AT ST ANDREWS. 26/04/2005

COLIN MONTGOMERIE ON THE 10TH TEE DURING THE SECOND ROUND OF THE JOHNNIE WALKER CHAMPIONSHIP AT
GLENEAGLES, PERTHSHIRE. 23/06/2006

USA'S DAVIS LOVE III PLAYS OUT OF A GREENSIDE BUNKER AT THE 13TH GREEN DURING A PRACTICE SESSION AT ROYAL LIVERPOOL GOLF CLUB, HOYLAKE. 17/07/2006

BRADLEY DREDGE (L) AND MARC WARREN ON THE THIRD DURING THE JOHNNIE WALKER CHAMPIONSHIP AT GLENEAGLES. 31/08/2007

SOUTH AFRICA'S ERNIE ELS WALKS TO
THE EIGHTH GREEN AT WENTWORTH.
13/10/2007

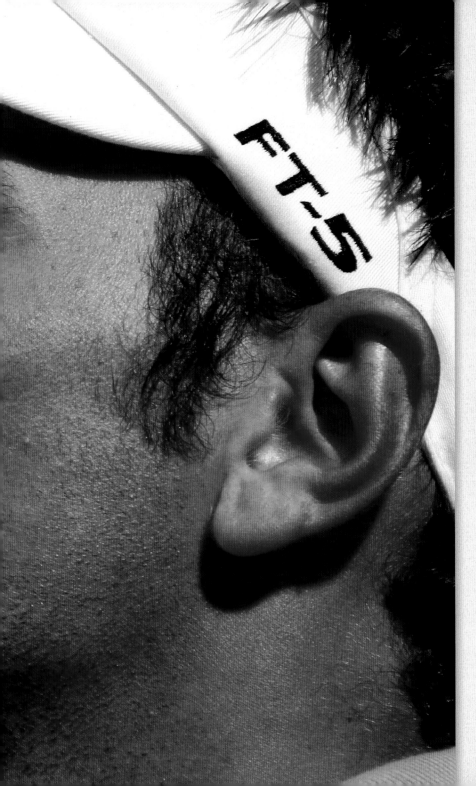

Chapter Three

MOMENTS

TRIUMPHS & DEFEATS

Anyone who has played golf knows what a frustrating game it can be; one minute you play the perfect shot, the next you are up to your knees in a ditch trying to find your ball

There is a thin line separating triumph and defeat, something one of the great players of the early 20th century, Harry Vardon, found out at the 1902 Open Championship at Hoylake. He needed only two fours over the last two holes to tie with Alex 'Sandy' Herd. His penultimate putt on the 18th green looked to be going in but at the last moment stopped right on the edge of the hole. A gust of wind would have blown it in, but when one needs the wind the air is always still...

That was Herd's first and only win in the Open, and two years later Jack White also upstaged the 'Great Triumvirate' of James Braid, J.H. Taylor and Harry Vardon when winning at Sandwich. On the way to victory he became the first player to break the 300 barrier in the tournament with a four-round total of 296.

Possibly the most remarkable Open victory of the early years of the century was that achieved by Scotland's George Duncan in 1920, the first championship after the Great War. He was 13 shots adrift of the leader Abe Mitchell after two rounds but by the end of the third he had made up the deficit.

The dramatic turnaround was attributed to the purchase of a new driver by Duncan after his two rounds of 80. That was not the only amazing comeback achieved during his career as seven years later, when playing in the

Irish Open at Portmarnock, he was 14 shots adrift of the leader in the last round but still came back to win.

The greatest force in women's golf at the time was Joyce Wethered who won the British Ladies' Amateur Golf Championship four times during the decade, and was English Ladies' champion for five consecutive years.

Although the 1930s heralded the arrival of Henry Cotton who won his first Open in 1934, it was also the decade when there were a remarkable four golfers who would each win the Championship just once in their careers: Alf Perry (1935), Alf Padgham (1936), Reg Whitcombe (1938) and Richard Burton (1939).

The Walker Cup, a competition for amateur golfers representing Great Britain and Ireland against the United States, was won for the first time by the GB team in 1938.

THE RYDER CUP

A similar contest for the professionals, the Ryder Cup, was begun in 1927 and

in the early years it resulted in some very exciting battles. Particularly in 1929 when 10,000 fans flocked to Moortown Golf Club in Leeds to see the famous Americans in action. Captain of the British side was George Duncan, who had to face the great Walter Hagen in a singles match. Apparently he was spurred on to victory after overhearing Gene Sarazen tell Hagen that he thought he was guaranteed a point against the Brit. That motivated Duncan, who led his team to a seven points to five victory. There was also a dramatic finish to the 1933 Cup when the two sides met at Southport. Although the home side were without the inspira-

ABOVE
THE TWO CAPTAINS, HENRY COTTON OF GREAT BRITAIN (L) AND USA'S LLOYD MANGRUM (R), SHOW OFF THE RYDER CUP. 29/09/1953

OPPOSITE
OPEN CHAMPION HENRY COTTON MAKES HIS ACCEPTANCE SPEECH AFTER COLLECTING THE CLARET JUG. 02/07/1948

tional Henry Cotton they were a tough proposition in their own backyard. However, it all came down to the final

match between American Herman Densmore Shute and Sid Easterbrook. Shute had a putt to win the match but missed two in succession to give Easterbrook a putt to win which he duly sunk from three feet to reclaim the Cup that the US had won two years earlier.

POST-WAR YEARS

After the Second World War the US were to dominate the competition and although it was a close run thing in 1953, that year's battle at Wentworth in Surrey ended up a disastrous one for the Brits.

Making his debut in the contest, Peter Alliss had a crucial match against Jim Turnesa in the singles. He was losing by just one hole but was in a good position as they approached the 18th hole. However, he took four shots from the fringe of the green and lost his match.

Bernard Hunt could have saved the day with a putt from four feet that would have drawn the contest but the pressure proved too much, he missed

and the US kept their hold on the trophy. Revenge came four years later at Lindrick in Yorkshire when Britain was led by Welshman Dai Rees. The home side rallied to win five of the seven singles matches.

Henry Cotton's final win in the Open came in 1948. When Max Faulkner won the contest three years later it was said that such was his confidence in victory, when he was two or three shots ahead he was signing the books of autograph hunters: 'Open champion 1951'.

TONY JACKLIN

Arguably the greatest golfing achievement of the 20th century was that of Scunthorpe-born Tony Jacklin. Not

only did he become the first British winner of the Open for 18 years following Faulkner, he went on to land the US version a year later in 1970 by seven strokes, the first Briton to do so since 1920.

PETER OOSTERHUIS

After a brilliant amateur career Peter Oosterhuis looked the man to follow in the footsteps of Jacklin when he won the European Order of Merit title four years in a row from 1971 to 1974, and he went close on two occasions when finishing runner-up in both 1974 and 1982.

The tall Londoner also suffered agonising defeats in the Open and the US Masters after leading in both.

THE 1980S ONWARDS

Paul Way won the 1985 British PGA Championship and two years later the European Open. Way was part of the victorious Europe team of 1985 although it all came down to Scotsman Sam Torrance. He faced US Open champion Andy North and soon fell behind. However, he fought back and it was neck-and-neck going to the 18th. North hits his ball into water, which left Torrance to hole out an 18-footer to win the match and the Ryder Cup, which he did comfortably.

Torrance also captained the European team to victory in the Ryder cup in 2002.

BRITISH MASTERY

Between 1988 and 1991 inclusive an Englishman (Nick Faldo twice), a Scotsman (Sandy Lyle) and a Welshman (Ian Woosnam) won the US Masters in Georgia, Atlanta, one of the four major titles in golf.

Faldo won that tournament again in 1996 when he got the better of an enthralling battle with Australian Greg Norman. Woosnam also captained the successful 2006 European team in the Ryder Cup.

WINNING RUN

One of the most extraordinary winning runs of the late 1990s was that of Lee Westwood. Over a twelve-month period starting in November 1997 he won an impressive eight tournaments worldwide, including first-time wins in America and Britain. Unsurprisingly, perhaps, he also won the Australian Open in Melbourne when beating Greg Norman in a play-off.

ABOVE
LEE WESTWOOD.

LEFT
THE RYDER CUP TROPHY.
23/09/1993

OPPOSITE
TONY JACKLIN PLAYS OUT OF THE ROUGH DURING THE OPEN AT ROYAL LYTHAM & ST ANNES.
12/07/1969

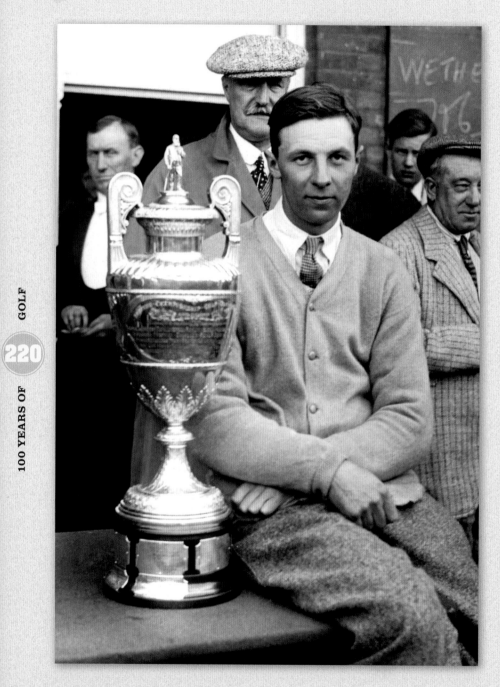

BRITISH AMATEUR CHAMPION ROGER
WETHERED WITH THE TROPHY.
12/05/1923

OPEN CHAMPION TOMMY ARMOUR
POSES WITH THE CLARET JUG FOR
THE PRESS. 06/06/1931

OPEN CHAMPION BOBBY LOCKE
WITH THE CLARET JUG. 09/07/1949

OPPOSITE

MILDRED 'BABE' ZAHARIAS POSES WITH THE TROPHY AFTER WINNING THE
LADIES' AMATEUR OPEN CHAMPIONSHIP. 12/06/1947

OPEN CHAMPION PETER THOMSON CELEBRATES WITH THE CLARET JUG. 06/07/1955

BOBBY LOCKE (L) IS INTERVIEWED
AFTER WINNING THE OPEN.
05/07/1957

GREAT BRITAIN CAPTAIN DAI REES (L) CONGRATULATES HIS FOURSOMES PARTNER KEN BOUSFIELD (R) AFTER THE LATTER SANK THE WINNING PUTT TO EARN BRITAIN'S ONLY FOURSOMES POINT IN THE RYDER CUP. 04/10/1957

MEMBERS OF THE VICTORIOUS
BRITISH RYDER CUP TEAM CHAIR
THEIR CAPTAIN DAI REES, AS HE
HOLDS ALOFT THE TROPHY.
05/10/1957

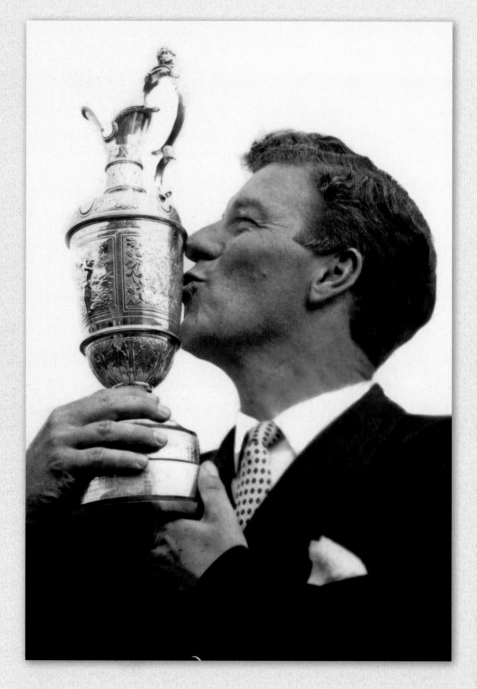

PETER THOMSON OF AUSTRALIA
KISSES THE TROPHY AFTER WINNING
THE OPEN CHAMPIONSHIP AT ROYAL
LYTHAM & ST ANNES. 1958

PETER THOMSON, OPEN CHAMPION
FOR THE FOURTH TIME, HOLDS
ALOFT THE TROPHY AT ROYAL
LYTHAM & ST ANNES. 1958

GARY PLAYER HOLDS UP THE TROPHY AFTER HIS WIN IN THE OPEN CHAMPIONSHIP. 03/07/1959

AMERICAN ARNOLD PALMER HOLDS THE OPEN CHAMPIONSHIP TROPHY, WHICH HE WON BY ONE STROKE FROM
WELSHMAN DAI REES. 15/07/1961

PROFESSIONAL GOLFERS ASSOCIATION
SCORE BOARD
DUNLOP-MASTERS
NAME
1 2 3 4 TOTAL
HITCHCOCK. J. 73 68 75 70 286
HUGGETT. B.G.C. 69 74 71 69 283
HUNT. B.J. 67 73 78
KING. S.L. 77 72 76 70
LEES. A. 72 73 74 66
LOCKE. A.D.A. 71 71
MIGUEL. A.G. 71 75
MILLER. D. 70
MOFFITT. R.L. 71 73
NAME
1 2 3 4 TOTAL
O'CONNOR. C. 73 70 69 72 284
PANTON. J. 71 69 69 73 282
PHILLIPS. F. 73 71 68 78 290
POVALL. Mr J. 75 70 77 83 305
REES. D.J. 71 66 70 71 278
SCOTT. S.S. 71 75 76 74 296
WHITEHEAD. E.R.A.
WILKES. B.

BOB CHARLES HOLDS THE TROPHY ALOFT AFTER WINNING THE OPEN CHAMPIONSHIP AT ROYAL LYTHAM & ST ANNES. 13/07/1963

OPPOSITE

DAI REES GIVES HIS ACCEPTANCE SPEECH AFTER WINNING THE DUNLOP MASTERS. 12/08/1962

AMERICAN TONY LEMA HOLDS THE
TROPHY AFTER WINNING THE OPEN.
10/07/1964

PETER THOMSON HOLDS THE CLARET JUG AFTER WINNING THE OPEN FOR THE FIFTH TIME. 09/07/1965

THE USA RYDER CUP TEAM LINE UP WITH THEIR BAGS: (L-R) ARNOLD PALMER, TOMMY JACOBS, GENE LITTLER, DAVE MARR, TONY LEMA, CAPTAIN BYRON NELSON, JULIUS BOROS, DON JANUARY, JOHNNY POTT, KEN VENTURI, BILLY CASPER.
08/10/1965

THE GREAT BRITAIN RYDER CUP TEAM LINE UP WITH THEIR BAGS: (L-R) PETER BUTLER, NEIL COLES, PETER ALLISS, CHRISTY O'CONNOR, GEORGE WILL, LIONEL PLATTS, DAVE THOMAS, JIMMY HITCHCOCK, JIMMY MARTIN, BERNARD HUNT, CAPTAIN HARRY WEETMAN. 08/10/1965

USA'S JACK NICKLAUS DRIVES BACK TO THE 17TH FAIRWAY FROM THE CAR PARK DURING THE PICCADILLY TOURNAMENT AT WENTWORTH. 06/10/1966

JACK NICKLAUS SHAKES HANDS WITH
THE WINNER OF THE PICCADILLY
TOURNAMENT, GARY PLAYER (R).
08/10/1966

AMERICAN DOUG SANDERS PRESENTS GIRLFRIEND SCOTTY WITH A ROSE AT HOYLAKE. 15/07/1967

OPPOSITE

AN ELATED ROBERTO DE VICENZO HOLDS THE TROPHY ALOFT AFTER WINNING
THE OPEN AT THE ROYAL LIVERPOOL COURSE AT HOYLAKE. 16/07/1967

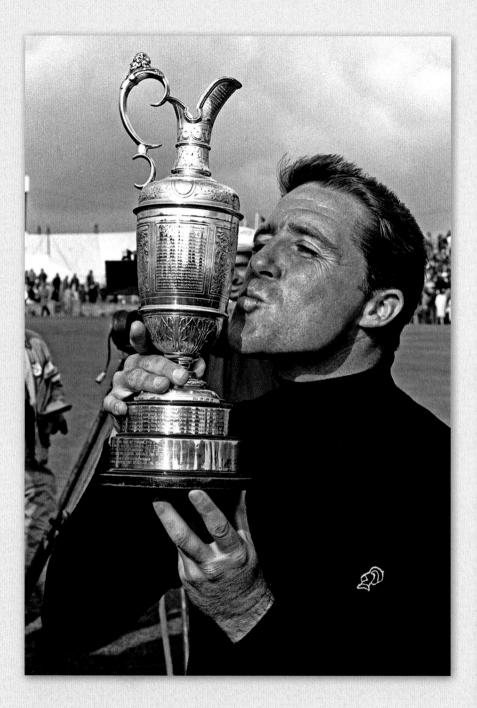

GARY PLAYER KISSES THE TROPHY
AFTER WINNING THE OPEN
CHAMPIONSHIP AT CARNOUSTIE,
ANGUS, REPEATING HIS TRIUMPH IN
THE 1959 COMPETITION. 13/07/1968

BOB CHARLES DRIVING OFF THE TEE AS TONY JACKLIN (L) WATCHES DURING THE OPEN AT ROYAL LYTHAM & ST ANNES.
12/07/1969

THE DAY AFTER WINNING THE OPEN CHAMPIONSHIP, TONY JACKLIN RELAXES WITH HIS TROPHY IN THE BACK GARDEN OF HIS FATHER, NEAR SCUNTHORPE, LINCOLNSHIRE. 13/07/1969

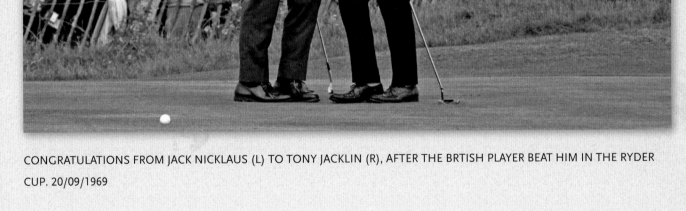

CONGRATULATIONS FROM JACK NICKLAUS (L) TO TONY JACKLIN (R), AFTER THE BRTISH PLAYER BEAT HIM IN THE RYDER CUP. 20/09/1969

JACK NICKLAUS ON THE 18TH IN THE OPEN CHAMPIONSHIP AT ST ANDREWS. 11/07/1970

DOUG SAUNDERS (L) AND JACK NICKLAUS (R) IN FINGER-TIP CONTACT AT ST ANDREWS WITH THE OPEN TROPHY THEY WERE SHARING FOR A FEW HOURS. CENTRE IS CABINET MINISTER WILLIE WHITELAW, WHO WAS CAPTAIN OF THE ROYAL AND ANCIENT GOLF CLUB. 11/07/1970

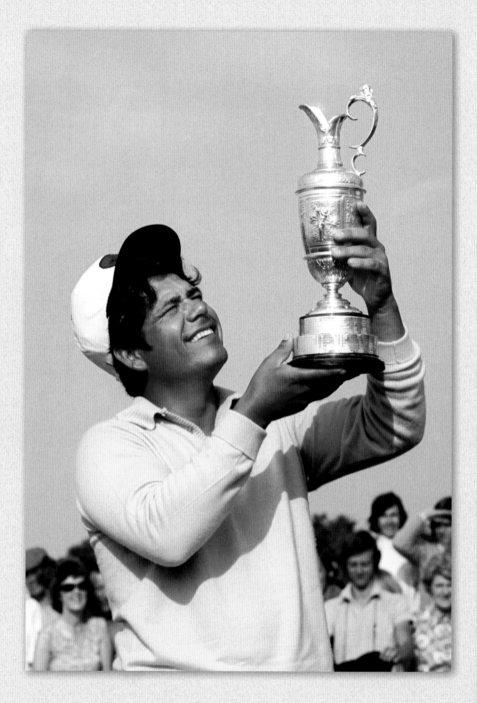

LEE TREVINO OF USA WITH THE
TROPHY AFTER WINNING THE OPEN
CHAMPIONSHIP AT MUIRFIELD.
15/07/1972

OPEN CHAMPION TOM WATSON (R) AND RUNNER UP JACK NEWTON (L) TRY TO FIX THE CLARET JUG BACK TO ITS BASE.
17/07/1975

OPEN CHAMPION JOHNNY MILLER (L)
WITH RUNNER UP SEVE BALLESTEROS
(R). 09/07/1976

JOHNNY MILLER CELEBRATES WITH THE CLARET JUG. 10/07/1976

TOM WATSON (USA) RAISES HIS HANDS IN TRIUMPH WALKING ONTO THE 18TH GREEN KNOWING HE HAS WON THE
OPEN CHAMPIONSHIP. 07/07/1977

OPEN CHAMPION JACK NICKLAUS
KEEPS A TIGHT GRIP ON THE CLARET
JUG. 15/07/1978

ISAO AOKI OF JAPAN HOLDS THE
TROPHY AND PRIZE CHEQUE AFTER
WINNING THE COLGATE WORLD
MATCHPLAY CHAMPIONSHIP AT
WENTWORTH. 16/10/1978

SEVE BALLESTEROS TAKES IT EASY AFTER WINNING HIS MATCH AGAINST BRITAIN'S BRIAN BARNES IN THE HENNESSY
COGNAC CUP AT SUNNINGDALE. 12/09/1980

OPEN CHAMPION TOM WATSON HOLDS UP A 'SCOTLAND THE BRAVE' SCARF DURING HIS VICTORY SPEECH. 20/07/1982

OPEN CHAMPION SEVE BALLESTEROS ADMIRES THE CLARET JUG AFTER HIS DRAMATIC VICTORY ON THE FINAL GREEN.
22/07/1984

SANDY LYLE KISSES THE OPEN
CHAMPIONSHIP TROPHY, AFTER
BECOMING THE FIRST BRITISH
PLAYER TO WIN THE TOURNAMENT
SINCE TONY JACKLIN IN 1969.
18/07/1985

THE EUROPEAN RYDER CUP TEAM AT THE BELFRY, SUTTON COLDFIELD: (L-R) IAN WOOSNAM, PAUL WAY, SAM TORRANCE, HOWARD CLARK, NICK FALDO, TONY JACKLIN, KEN BROWN, SANDY LYLE, BERNHARD LANGER, SEVE BALLESTEROS, JOSE-MARIA CANIZARES, MANUEL PINERO AND JOSE RIVERO. 11/09/1985

EUROPE CAPTAIN TONY JACKLIN (R) CONGRATULATES MANUEL PINERO (L) ON HIS VICTORY IN THE FIRST SINGLES MATCH OF THE LAST DAY OF THE RYDER CUP. 15/09/1985

OPPOSITE

VICTORIOUS CAPTAIN TONY JACKLIN HOLDS ALOFT THE RYDER CUP. 15/09/1985

SCOTLAND'S SAM TORRANCE
ACKNOWLEDGES THE CHEERING
CROWD AFTER HE SANK A 20FT PUTT
FOR A BIRDIE THREE TO SQUARE IN
THE MATCH AT THE NINTH AGAINST
AMERICAN TWOSOME RAY FLOYD
AND LARRY WATKINS. TORRANCE WAS
PARTNERED BY HOWARD CLARK IN
THE ROUND OF THE RYDER CUP AT
THE BELFRY. 16/09/1985

GREG NORMAN CELEBRATES AFTER
CHIPPING THE BALL IN FROM JUST
OFF THE GREEN DURING THE OPEN
AT TURNBERRY. 19/07/1986

NICK FALDO CELEBRATES WINNING
THE 116TH OPEN CHAMPIONSHIP AT
MUIRFIELD. 18/07/1987

OPPOSITE

GREG NORMAN KISSES THE OPEN TROPHY AFTER HIS VICTORY AT TURNBERRY. 20/07/1986

THE EUROPEAN TEAM POSE WITH THE RYDER CUP AT HEATHROW AIRPORT ON THEIR RETURN TO ENGLAND: (BACK, L-R) JOSE RIVERO, GORDON BRAND JR, SAM TORRANCE, IAN WOOSNAM; (MIDDLE, L-R) EAMONN DARCY, HOWARD CLARK, JOSE MARIA OLAZABAL (HIDDEN), BERNHARD LANGER, NICK FALDO; (FRONT, L-R) SEVE BALLESTEROS, CAPTAIN TONY JACKLIN. 28/09/1987

DURING THE OPEN, SEVE
BALLESTEROS CELEBRATES AFTER
JUDGING HIS CHIP FROM THE EDGE
OF THE 18TH GREEN TO PERFECTION.
16/07/1988

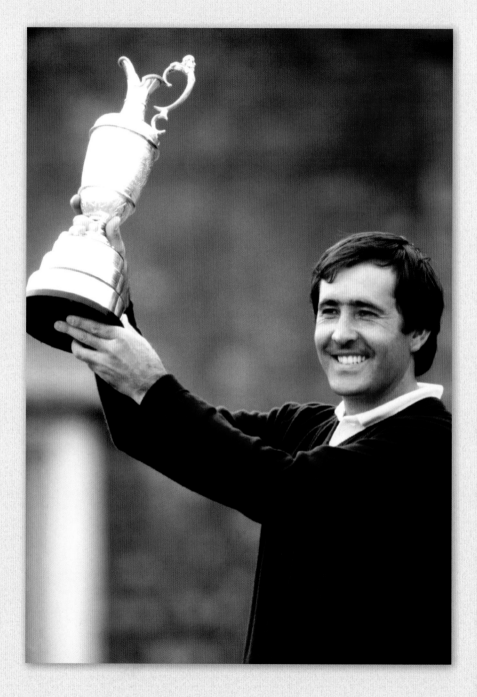

OPEN CHAMPION SEVE BALLESTEROS
LIFTS THE CLARET JUG. 16/07/1988

IAN WOOSNAM POSES WITH THE
PANASONIC EUROPEAN OPEN
TROPHY. 11/09/1988

EUROPE'S CHRISTY O'CONNOR JNR (C) COMMISERATES WITH USA'S FRED COUPLES (R) AFTER BEATING HIM IN THE RYDER CUP, WHILE O'CONNOR'S CADDY (L) CELEBRATES. 24/09/1989

CHRISTY O'CONNOR CELEBRATES AFTER HIS PUTT ON THE 18TH HOLE WON THE RYDER CUP FOR EUROPE. 24/09/1989

JOY FOR NICK FALDO AFTER HE HAD
SUNK THE 20FT PUTT ON THE LAST
GREEN WHICH GAVE HIM VICTORY IN
THE SUNTORY WORLD MATCH PLAY
CHAMPIONSHIP AT WENTWORTH.
15/10/1989

NICK FALDO SITTING ON THE SWILKAN BRIDGE ON THE 18TH FAIRWAY OF ST. ANDREWS WITH THE OPEN TROPHY.

23/07/1990

NICK FALDO, HIS WIFE GILL (R) AND CADDY FANNY SUNESSON SALUTE FANS AT THE 18TH AFTER FALDO WON THE 121ST OPEN CHAMPIONSHIP AT MUIRFIELD. 19/07/1992

GARY EVANS CELEBRATES GETTING OUT OF A BUNKER BY THE SIXTH GREEN DURING THE SECOND DAY OF THE OPEN
TOURNAMENT AT ROYAL ST GEORGE'S. 16/07/1993

USA'S FRED COUPLES AND EUROPE'S IAN WOOSNAM FINISH ALL SQUARE AFTER THEIR ROUND IN THE RYDER CUP.

26/09/1993

DESPAIR FOR EUROPE'S CONSTANTINO ROCCA AFTER A POOR SHOT IN THE RYDER CUP. 26/09/1993

USA'S TOM WATSON AND HIS WIFE WATCH THE RYDER CUP ACTION FROM THE 18TH GREEN AT THE BELFRY. 26/09/1993

NICK PRICE HUGS THE TROPHY AFTER
WINNING THE OPEN. 17/07/1994

JOHN DALY CELEBRATES WITH HIS
WIFE DURING THE OPEN AS A
STREAKER RACES OFF IN THE
BACKGROUND. 23/07/1995

IAN WOOSNAM JUST MISSES A PUTT IN HIS MATCH WITH FRED COUPLES IN THE RYDER CUP. 24/09/1995

PHILIP WALTON CELEBRATES AFTER HIS PUTT WON EUROPE THE RYDER CUP AGAINST USA IN ROCHESTER, NY. 24/09/1995

NICK FALDO SINKS TO THE FLOOR AS
A GIRL MAKES HER WAY OFF THE
FAIRWAY AFTER GIVING HIM A ROSE
AT THE OPEN IN ST ANDREWS.
26/09/1995

EUROPE'S RYDER CUP CAPTAIN SEVE BALLESTEROS (C) SHARES A JOKE WITH TEAMMATE NICK FALDO (SECOND RIGHT) AT THE TEAM PICTURE SESSION. 24/09/1997

OPPOSITE

AMERICAN TOM LEHMAN HUGS THE OPEN CHAMPIONSHIP TROPHY

AT ROYAL LYTHAM & ST ANNES. 21/07/1996

EUROPE'S TRIUMPHANT CAPTAIN
SEVE BALLESTEROS HOLDS THE
RYDER CUP ALOFT. 28/09/1997

OPEN CHAMPION MARK O'MEARA

HOLDS THE CLARET JUG ALOFT.

19/07/1998

JUSTIN LEONARD CELEBRATES SINKING HIS PUTT DURING THE RYDER CUP. 26/09/1999

BEN CRENSHAW CELEBRATES WINNING THE RYDER CUP AND GIVES THE THUMBS UP TO THE AMERICAN FANS. 26/09/1999

SCOTLAND'S SAM TORRANCE DURING A PHOTOCALL AT WENTWORTH, WHERE HE WAS CONFIRMED AS EUROPE'S RYDER CUP CAPTAIN. 01/12/1999

EUROPE CAPTAIN SAM TORRANCE
HOLDS THE RYDER CUP ON THE 10TH
GREEN BRIDGE AT THE BELFRY.
30/09/2002

USA'S JACK NICKLAUS WAVES TO THE CROWDS ON THE 18TH HOLE DURING THE OPEN AT ST ANDREWS. 15/07/2005

OPPOSITE

ENGLAND'S IAN POULTER (L), LEE WESTWOOD AND SCOTLAND'S COLIN
MONTGOMERIE ON THE SEVENTH FAIRWAY DURING THE DAILY TELEGRAPH
DUNLOP MASTERS. 13/05/2005

TIGER WOODS, US RYDER CUP TEAM, DURING PRACTICE. 20/09/2006

EUROPEAN RYDER CUP PLAYER, SERGIO GARCIA, CONTEMPLATES A PUTT DURING HIS FINAL PRACTICE ROUND AT THE K CLUB, CO KILDARE, AHEAD OF THE RYDER CUP. 21/09/2006

DARREN CLARKE CELEBRATES EUROPE'S WIN IN THE RYDER CUP. 24/09/2006

OPPOSITE

EUROPE'S LUKE DONALD CELEBRATES AFTER DEFEATING USA'S CHAD CAMPBELL
AT THE 17TH HOLE DURING DAY THREE OF THE RYDER CUP. 24/09/2006

GREGORY HAVRET WITH THE TROPHY AFTER WINNING THE BARCLAYS SCOTTISH OPEN AT LOCH LOMOND. 15/07/2007

NICK DOUGHERTY KISSES THE TROPHY AFTER WINNING THE ALFRED DUNHILL LINKS CHAMPIONSHIP AT ST ANDREWS.
07/10/2007

The Publishers gratefully acknowledge PA Photos, from whose extensive archive – including The Press Association, Barratts and Sport & General collections – the photographs in this book have been selected.

Personal copies of the photographs in this book, and many others, may be ordered online at www.prints.paphotos.com

AMMONITE
PRESS

For more information, please contact:

AMMONITE PRESS

AE Publications Ltd. 166 High Street, Lewes, East Sussex, BN7 1XU, United Kingdom
Tel: 01273 488005 Fax: 01273 402866
www.ae-publications.com